SHAWN MENDES

CANADIAN SINGER

MR VIVEK KUMAR PANDEY

Made with ♥ on the Notion Press Platform
www.notionpress.com

Contents

Foreword *v*

Preface *vii*

1. Shawn Mendes 1

2. Cinema Of Canada 17

Foreword

During Writing This Book No Character No Religion Are Harmed It's Only For Study Purpose.We don't want to hurt anyone. In This Book There Is Short Biography Of Canadian Singer Shawn Mendes & It's Life Style,Achievement,etc.

Preface

Author biography in English :

MY NAME IS VIVEK KUMAR PANDEY . I WAS BORN IN 30 SEP 2002,I AM FROM SURAT GUJARAT INDIA.MY DREAM WAS TO BE GOOD WRITERS ,MY FAMILY SUPPORTED ME TO SUCCESSFUL AND I CAN DO IT MY SELF.How do I write? That is a question, I believe, that can be honestly answered by me."CELEBRATING YOUNGEST WRITER AWARD WINNER IN GUJARAT 1ST RANK" MR PANDEY JI . I may think I did a good job writing something. The reader is the one who decides the quality of my writing. I do find writing to be natural to me and therefore find it to be a real challenge. My trick as a challenged writer is to do the best I can and know that I am happy with the final outcome. It may take a while to do my best and there may be quite a few problems I run into along the way.

I am not a greedy person those who are thinking about me and my self I never tried it anyone people suffering from sadness ,I trying to get promoted people suffering from happiness and joy in your Life Time. Now in current situation in India and also world people are unemployed and have no many but our indian governor help to people to get free food from ration card , i also take part in leadership team ,i am Motivational speaker , Film script writer. There was my two dream firstly writer and secondly actor & also my own film is upcoming soon i done almost completely completed script for my film .I AM GOING TO SAY WORD OF HEART TOUCH OUT PLEASE READ IT" , firstly i thanks my father he supports me in this field they always getting inspired me by own his words and behavior ,they always said that he was a biggest person in the world in future and also they purchase fruit and chocolate for me in anytime & anyway , firstly my father buy him then call me Vivek you want a chocolate i will say yes papa but how many tell me ,papa: you tell me how much i buy him i told 1 or 2 chocolate but my father purchase whole the boxes of chocolate and they get suprised me. MY FATHER WAS BORN IN " 20 SEPTEMBER" 1971 IN INDIA.

1) MY FATHER FAVORITE CLOTHES IS KURTA PAIJMA AND ALSO STYLES SHOE

2) FAVORITE SINGER IS KISHORE DA

3) FAVORITE STATE GUJARAT AND KOLKATA , HIS VILLAGE IN BIHAR

4) FAVORITE COLOR BLACK AND WHITE

THEY ALSO LOVE cricket like IPL and one day t-20 .they also like watching a News daily and heard the song daily ,they also interested in tik tok video but in current time tik tok is banned in india but also few videos are in you tube. In lockdown time my family and me very enjoy day daily. my father play daily ludo with his sister and son, daughter.they always loved tea and coffee anytime call me ". I make it tea for my father but some reason after the April to june they are suffering from fever and cough , weakness on 6 June 2020 my father death. they not told me say bye bye his life. After death of 6 June on 10 june my mom and dad anniversary.but my father is Best in the world they can do anything for me please take care of father and respect it of your parents.

CHAPTER ONE

Shawn Mendes

- **Shawn Mendes**

1. During Writing This Book No Character No Religion Are Harmed It's Only For Study Purpose.We don't want to hurt anyone. In This Book There Is Short Biography Of Canadian Singer Shawn Mendes & It's Life Style,Achievement,etc.

Shawn Peter Raul Mendes (born August 8, 1998) is a Canadian singer and songwriter. He gained a following in 2013, posting song covers on the video-sharing application Vine. The following year, he caught the attention of artist manager Andrew Gertler and Island Records A&R Ziggy Chareton, which led to him signing a deal with the record label. Mendes's self-titled debut EP was released in 2014, followed by his debut studio album Handwritten in 2015. Handwritten debuted atop the US Billboard 200, making Mendes one of five artists ever to debut at number one before the age of 18. The single "Stitches" reached number one in the UK and the top 10 in the US and Canada.

His second studio album Illuminate (2016) also debuted at number one in the US, with its singles "Treat You Better" and "There's Nothing Holdin‘ Me Back" reaching the top 10 in several countries. His self-titled third studio album (2018) was supported by the lead single "In My Blood". The album's number one debut in the US made Mendes the third-youngest artist to achieve three number one albums. In 2019, he released the hit singles "If I Can't Have You" and "Señorita", with the latter peaking atop the US Billboard Hot 100. His fourth studio album, Wonder (2020), made Mendes the youngest male artist ever to top the Billboard 200 with four studio albums.

Among his accolades, Mendes has won 13 SOCAN awards, 10 MTV Europe Music Awards, eight Juno Awards, eight iHeartRadio MMVAs, two American Music Awards, and received three nominations for a Grammy Award and one nomination for a Brit Award. In 2018, Time named Mendes as one of the 100 most influential people in the world on their annual list.

- Shawn Mendes life and education

Shawn Peter Raul Mendes was born and raised in Pickering, Ontario, to Karen Mendes, a real estate agent, and Manuel Mendes, a businessman, who sells bar and restaurant supplies in Toronto. His father is from Algarve, Portugal, while his mother is from England. He has a younger sister named Aaliyah. He was raised in a religious family.He played youth soccer with Pickering FC.

Mendes graduated from Pine Ridge Secondary School in June 2016, where he played ice hockey and soccer, joined his high school glee club, and practised his stage presence in acting lessons (leading as Prince Charming at one point). He also auditioned for Disney Channel in Toronto.

- Shawn Mendes Career

Mendes learned to play guitar by watching YouTube tutorial videos at the age of 14 in 2012.Less than a year later he started posting cover videos on YouTube. Mendes started attracting viewers after he posted a cover from Justin Bieber's "As Long as You Love Me" on the social video app Vine in 2013 and got 10,000 likes and as many followers the next day. After that he gained millions of views and followers in a few months, becoming well known for his six-second snippets of renditions of many popular songs.

Mendes saw Bieber as a career model at the time. By August 2014, he was the third most-followed musician on Vine. Artist manager Andrew Gertler discovered Mendes online in November 2013, bringing him to Island Records in January 2014. In April, he won Ryan Seacrest's "Best Cover Song" contest with "Say Something" by A Great Big World. He officially signed to Island in May 2014.

He released his first single "Life of the Party" on June 26, 2014.He became the youngest to debut in the top 25 on the US Billboard Hot 100, making it to number 24 for the week ending July 12, 2014. Prior to his signing, Mendes toured as a member of the Magcon Tour alongside other young Viners with a large following on social media.

Mendes was also on a nationwide tour with Austin Mahone as an opening act. He released his debut major label EP in July. The EP debuted and peaked at number five on the Billboard 200, selling 48,000 copies in its first week. He won a Teen Choice award in 2014 for Webstar in Music. On September 5, 2014, "Oh Cecilia (Breaking My Heart)" featuring Mendes was released as the fifth single from The Vamps' debut album, Meet the Vamps. On November 6,

2014, "Something Big" was released as the second single.

On April 14, 2015, Mendes released his full-length album Handwritten, which debuted at number one on the Billboard 200 chart with 119,000 equivalent album units, selling 106,000 copies in its first week and was certified platinum. Mendes then became the youngest artist to debut at number one since the release of Justin Bieber's My World 2.0.

The third single from the album, "Stitches", peaked at number four on the US Billboard Hot 100, becoming his first top 10 single in the US, and became his first number one on the Adult Pop Songs and Adult Contemporary charts. The song later reached number one in the UK. Also in 2015, Mendes opened for Taylor Swift during 1989 World Tour dates for North America and recorded "Believe" for the soundtrack of Disney Channel Original Movie Descendants. In late 2015, Mendes and Camila Cabello, who was at the time a member of the group Fifth Harmony, released their collaborative single "I Know What You Did Last Summer". The song was included on Mendes' Handwritten Revisited reissue.

Mendes was listed among Time's "25 Most Influential Teens of 2014", debuting in the list after being the youngest-ever artist to debut in the top 25 of Billboard Hot 100. He was listed in Time's "The 30 Most Influential Teens of 2015", making the list after his debut album topped the Billboard 200 and his single "Stitches" made the top 10 in the US and other countries.

- Shawn Mendes in 2017

On January 21, 2016, Mendes made his acting debut on The CW's The 100 third-season premiere. He later announced his second world tour as a headliner, the Shawn Mendes World Tour, which started in March 2016 and sold out 38 shows in North America and Europe within minutes.Mendes released "Treat You Better", the lead single from his second studio album, in June 2016. In the US, the single reached the top 10 on the Billboard Hot 100, became his second single to peak atop both the Adult Contemporary and Adult Pop Songs chart, and was certified triple platinum. It also went top 10 in the UK.

The album, Illuminate, was released on September 23, 2016, and debuted at number one on the US Billboard 200 with 145,000 equivalent album units, including 121,000 in pure album sales and was certified platinum. It debuted atop the charts in Canada, becoming his second number one album in his home country. "Mercy" was released as the second single on August 18, 2016, which entered the top 20 in the US and the UK and was certified double platinum. Mendes released the live album Live at Madison Square Garden in December 2016.He appeared as the musical guest on Saturday Night Live, December 3, 2016.

In April 2017, Mendes embarked on his Illuminate World Tour, which sold-out arenas around the world such as Los Angeles' Staples Center and London's The O2 Arena. He released the single "There's Nothing Holdin‘ Me Back" on April 20, 2017, included on his Illuminate deluxe edition. The song was Mendes' third single to reach the top 10 in the US and third single to reach number one on both the Adult Contemporary and Adult Pop Songs chart. In August 2017, he became the first artist under 20 years old to have three number-one songs on the Billboard Adult Pop Songs chart. In November 2017, Mendes became the first artist to have three number-one songs on the Billboard Adult Contemporary chart before turning 20 years old, an unprecedented feat since the founding of the chart more than 50 years ago.

Mendes was listed among Time's The 30 Most Influential Teens of 2016 and made his first appearance on Forbes's 30 Under 30 2016: Music. He topped Billboard's 21 Under 21 list in 2017, after his two albums topped the Billboard 200 and his single "There's Nothing Holding Me Back" became his fifth top 20 on the Billboard Hot 100.

- Shawn Mendes performs "In My Blood" at the 2018

On March 22, 2018, Mendes released the lead single "In My Blood" from his upcoming third studio album, followed up by the second single "Lost in Japan" on March 23. "In My Blood" topped the Billboard Adult Pop Songs chart, making Mendes the first and only artist to have four number one singles in the chart before turning 20 years old. "Youth" was released on May 3, featuring American singer Khalid. His self-titled studio album was released on May 25, 2018, to positive critical reviews, with particular praise towards his songwriting and artistic growth. It debuted at number one in Canada, making it his third number one album in his home country. It debuted at number one on the US Billboard 200, making Mendes the third-youngest artist to collect three number-one albums.

Mendes performing at the concert honouring the 92nd birthday of Elizabeth II in April 2018 .To promote the album, Mendes embarked on his self-titled world tour in 2019. Besides the tour, he performed at music festivals across Europe, North America, and South America. He performed at a televised concert honouring the 92nd birthday of Queen Elizabeth II on April 21, 2018. He made TV show appearances on The Late Late Show with James

Corden in June where he sang one of his latest singles each night for a week. The tracks he performed live were "Nervous", "Lost in Japan", "Perfectly Wrong", and the duet with Julia Michaels "Like to be You".

Mendes made an appearance on the late-night talk show The Tonight Show Starring Jimmy Fallon in October and performed Lost in Japan. He, together with Fallon and the show's resident band The Roots, performed a special version of "Treat You Better" for the show's Classroom Instruments series. He has also performed his latest singles on the iHeartRadio MMVAs in Canada on August 27, where he received eight nominations and won four awards.

Mendes starred in a documentary directed by YouTube star Casey Neistat. The short film is part of YouTube's Artist Spotlight Story series, featuring an interview with Mendes and backstage and behind-the-scene footage of Mendes during one of his tours. The trailer was released on YouTube on September 22 to officially announce the upcoming documentary. The documentary, Shawn Mendes – Artist Spotlight Stories, was published on September 28. Ahead of the official release day, Mendes and Neistat held a previewing show of the film where selected fans of Mendes were invited for the event.

The remixed version of "Lost in Japan", by Russian-German DJ Zedd, was released on September 27. Mendes performed the remix version of the single during the 2018 American Music Award held in Los Angeles on October 9.He was joined onstage by Zedd. Mendes was listed on Billboard "21 Under 21 2018", topping the list for the second year in a row for his chart performance, having three consecutive number one albums.

Mendes and Zac Brown Band were featured in an episode of the American TV program CMT Crossroads, a show that pairs a country musician with a musician from another genre. The episode was aired on October 24 and was taped a month before the scheduled airing date. Mendes and Zac Brown Band performed nine songs, where they sang parts of each other's songs and covered Michael Jackson's "Man in the Mirror". Parts of the dialogue between Mendes and Zac Brown Band, talking about music and experiences throughout their career, were shown in between the song performances.

- Shawn Mendes at the November 2019 American Music Awards

On November 1, Mendes was announced as one of the musical performers for the 2018 Victoria's Secret Fashion Show which was recorded in New York City in November and aired in December. He released a three-song remix EP on December 21 entitled The Album (Remixes). The EP includes remixes of songs from his self-titled album such as "Where Were You in the Morning?" with Kaytranada, "Why" with Leon Bridges, and "Youth" with Jessie Reyez.

On May 3, 2019, Mendes released the single "If I Can't Have You" along with its music video. The single debuted at number two in the US Billboard Hot 100, becoming his highest-charting single on the chart. It also debuted in the top 10 in Australia and the UK, becoming his fifth top 10 single in both countries. On July 19, he released the Gryffin remix of "If I Can't Have You". On June 21, 2019, he released "Señorita" with Cuban singer Camila Cabello, along with the music video. The song debuted at number two on the US Billboard Hot 100 chart and marks Mendes and Cabello's second collaboration, following "I Know What You Did Last Summer" released in 2015. On August

26, 2019, "Señorita" peaked at number one, making it Mendes‘ first chart-topping single on the Hot 100.The deluxe edition of Shawn Mendes was released on July 27, 2019, and includes the songs "If I Can't Have You" and "Señorita".

- Shawn Mendes speaking to Vanity Fair in 2020

On September 30, 2020, Mendes announced that his fourth studio album, Wonder, would be released on December 4, along with announcing that the album's lead single, also called "Wonder", would be released on October 2. Through promotional videos, "Intro", the first song from the album, was also released. "Wonder" debuted and peaked at number 18 on the US Billboard Hot 100.On October 13, Mendes announced that a documentary titled Shawn Mendes: In Wonder, which chronicles the past few years of his life, would be released on Netflix on November 23. A concert film titled, "Shawn Mendes: Live in Concert", was also released on Netflix on November 25, following his first ever performance at the Rogers Centre on September 6, 2019.

On November 16, 2020, Mendes announced a that the second single from Wonder was a collaboration with Justin Bieber on a track entitled "Monster". The single and the music video were released on November 20, 2020.The song peaked at number eight on the US Billboard Hot 100. Mendes performed "Monster" live for the first time with Bieber at the 2020 American Music Awards; he also performed "Wonder". On December 4, the album Wonder was released, debuting at number one in the US as well as Canada. On December 6, Mendes held a concert event titled, Wonder: The Experience, where he did a Q&A

session, performed songs from the album, and talked about the behind the scenes of making of the record.On December 7, Mendes did an interview alongside Matthew McConaughey and performed "Dream" for the first time on television during his appearance on The Late Late Show.

On August 20, 2021, Mendes released "Summer of Love" with Tainy. That same month, it was announced that Mendes would serve as an executive producer – via his production banner, Permanent Content – for Legendary's TV adaptation of Square Enix's video game Life Is Strange.

On September 23, 2021, Mendes announced that he would be embarking on Wonder: The World Tour, across North America, the United Kingdom, and Europe, consisting of 64 dates and starting on March 14, 2022, at the Royal Arena in Copenhagen. He performed seven shows before postponing three weeks due to his mental health before eventually cancelling the remaining eighty scheduled shows. Mendes stated he would continue to make music and that he hopes to tour again.

On November 30, 2021, Mendes announced a new single, titled "It'll Be Okay", would be released on December 1. On March 20, 2022, he premiered a new song titled "When You're Gone" during his performance.

Mendes has mainly been described as a pop and folk-pop singer. Mendes has cited John Mayer, Ed Sheeran, Taylor Swift, Justin Timberlake, and Bruno Mars as his main musical influences.Growing up, Mendes listened to reggae music, Led Zeppelin, Garth Brooks, and country music thanks to his parents. He expressed that his second studio album was influenced by Mayer's workwhile his third album was inspired by Timberlake, Kings of Leon, Kanye West, and Daniel Caesar. For Brittany Spanos of Rolling Stone, Mendes incorporates "catchy acoustic folk-pop tunes" in his catalogue, while for Joe Coscarelli of The New York Times, "his soft, sometimes soulful pop-rock plays primarily to tweens and teenagers, but has also found traction on adult contemporary radio stations". In an interview with Clash magazine, Mendes stated:

"I want to create anthems for people. I want to create anthems for big moments in their lives.I don't want my music to play for a few months and then go away forever. And not only that, I want to do incredible things that make a difference too. I think it's not only about the music you release, it's about the things you do while you're making the music."

- Shawn Mendes signed with Wilhelmina Models in 2016.

In June 2017, Mendes walked the runway during the "Emporio Armani Spring 2018" show held in Milan, Italy. Mendes was wearing the Italian brand's new smartwatch, EA Connected, during the show. Ahead of his runway walk, the promotional video featuring Mendes was shown. In August 2017, Mendes launched his first fragrance, Shawn Mendes Signature, a fragrance for women and men. He launched his second fragrance, Shawn Signature II, also made for both men and women in August 2018.

On June 6, 2018, Mendes was announced as the ambassador for Emporio Armani's entire "Fall Winter 2018-2019" watch collection. In July 2018, photographs of Mendes wearing the new EA Connected smartwatches were published on social media.

On February 16, 2019, Mendes announced that he was the latest brand ambassador for Calvin Klein's #MyCalvins campaign. During the 61st Annual Grammy Awards, SmileDirectClub released an advertisement showcasing a campaign between the company and Mendes with some of the proceeds going to "organizations that seek to improve children's health as well as mental and emotional well-being." Later that month, Emporio Armani released a new black-and-white advertisement for its touchscreen smartwatches featuring an instrumental version of "In My Blood" with Mendes boxing.

In August 2019, Mendes announced a partnership with Canadian-based food chain, Tim Hortons, in which he features in a commercial and on beverage cups, followed by a partnership with Roots Canada in September.

- Notes from Shawn

In 2014, Mendes and DoSomething.org launched their campaign called "Notes from Shawn" where fans were encouraged to write positive notes and leave them in unexpected places. The campaign was inspired by the lyrics to his first single, "Life of the Party", and addressed low self-esteem, depression and awareness of self-harm. They relaunched their campaign for the second year in a row in 2015, where the campaign was hashtagged online as NotesFromShawn. He partnered with BlendApp with the goal of raising up to $25,000, where $1 was raised for every signup and positive message shared on the application. The campaign was relaunched for a third year in a row in 2016.

He has also worked with Pencils of Promise, a non-profit organization that builds schools and helps raise the quality of education for developing countries, raising $25,000 to build a school in Ghana.In September 2017, after witnessing the devastation of the earthquake in Mexico City, Mendes created the Mexico Earthquake Relief Fund in conjunction with the American Red Cross and donated $100,000 towards relief efforts.

In 2018, Mendes worked with Omaze to raise funds through donations to support the WE Schools program, a movement aiming to support youth through educational services and mentorship. Mendes encouraged his fans to help the cause while giving the donors a chance to attend his upcoming concert tour.

In September 2018, Mendes took part in the annual Global Citizen festival held at Central Park, New York City. He performed, alongside other artists such as Janelle Monáe, John Legend, and Janet Jackson, and raised awareness regarding the importance of education and children's lack of access to education around the world, particularly young women. Ahead of the event, he took to social media to reach out to Canada's Prime Minister Justin Trudeau, thanking the Prime Minister for leading the initiative for Leave No Girl Behind, a movement whose goal is to empower girls through workshops and programs, and expressing his willingness to talk more about the project. He also encouraged his fans to support the movement. In response, the Prime Minister thanked Mendes and stated that "The more people we have fighting for girls' education, the better! Let's talk."

In October 2018, Mendes, together with producer Teddy Geiger, released a cover of "Under Pressure" by the British rock band Queen and David Bowie. The single was part of a series of covers of Queen's songs, released in celebration of Queen's biopic Bohemian Rhapsody. The proceeds from the single were donated to the Mercury Phoenix Trust, an organization founded by Queen bandmembers after Freddie Mercury's death, which helps fight against HIV/AIDS. Queen's manager, Jim Beach, expressed his gratitude to Mendes and Universal Music

Group for helping the cause.

On October 20, 2018, Mendes performed along with other artists such as Khalid, NF, Marshmello, Meghan Trainor, and Ella Mai at The Hollywood Bowl, Los Angeles for the "We Can Survive" event. The event was organized to raise funds for Young Survival Coalition, in an effort to support young women who were diagnosed with breast cancer.

In August 2019, Mendes announced the launch of the Shawn Mendes Foundation, with the aim to "inspire and empower his fans and today's youth to bring about positive change in the world and advocate for issues they care most about." On 8 January 2020, Mendes announced that both he and his Shawn Mendes Foundation will be donating an undisclosed sum of money to causes including Australia's Red Cross, the New South Wales Rural Fire Service, and South Australia Country Fire Service, to help ease the strain on those impacted by the devastating fires that are tearing through parts of the country. In March 2020 Mendes and The Shawn Mendes Foundation donated $175,000 to support COVID-19 relief to Toronto's SickKids Foundation, the largest charitable funder of child health research, learning and care in Canada.

In March 2020, Mendes participated in iHeart Media's Living Room Concert for America, a benefit to raise awareness and funds for the COVID-19 pandemic. In March and April 2020, Mendes participated in Global Citizen Festival's Together at Home virtual concert to raise awareness and funds for the COVID-19 pandemic. Mendes has shown support for the Black Lives Matter movement. In May 2020 he alongside Camila Cabello joined protests in Miami for racial justice after the murder of George Floyd, and has had lent his Instagram to raise the voice of Black activists.

On April 22, 2021, Mendes hosted a NASA video conference with the crew of Expedition 65 on board the International Space Station. The televised event covered a Q&A with students and children about various topics related to Earth Day, such as climate change, Earth observations and general physics, as well as the astronauts' experience on the space station. In June 2021, Mendes, along with several other celebrities, signed an open letter to the United States Congress, urging lawmakers to pass the Equality Act. The artists, including Mendes, said of the Act that it would "protect ... the most marginalized communities".

In May 2021, Mendes joined Cabello and Bollywood actors to help fight the COVID-19 pandemic in India, during its peak of cases. Mendes donated $50,000 through the organization Give India.

- Shawn Mendes Personal life

Mendes has been open about his struggles with anxiety, which he disclosed publicly through "In My Blood", a track from his third studio album. He declared that he had been undergoing therapy in order to help him deal with the mental health condition, stating:

I spoke to a therapist a couple of times. Therapy is what works for you. Therapy is listening to music and running on the treadmill, therapy is going to dinner with your friends—it's something that distracts you, that helps you heal and so it just depends on what you think therapy is. I made a conscious effort to be more connected to the people in my life. I found I was closing myself off from everybody, thinking that would help me battle it then realizing the only way I was going to battle it was completely opening up and letting people in.

As of 2021, Mendes resides in a condominium in downtown TorontoRegarding speculations about his sexuality, Mendes said, "First of all, I'm not gay. Second of all, it shouldn't make a difference if I was or if I wasn't. The focus should be on the music and not my sexuality."Mendes began dating Cuban-American singer Camila Cabello in July 2019. Their relationship sparked controversy, as both were accused of attempting to form a relationship for publicity, but Mendes insisted it was "definitely not a publicity stunt". The couple announced their split in November 2021.

- Shawn Mendes achievements

Mendes has received several nominations and awards. He won 18 Society of Composers, Authors and Music Publishers of Canada (SOCAN) awards, twelve Juno Awards, eleven MTV Europe Music Awards (EMA), eight iHeartRadio Much Music Video Awards (MMVA), five BMI Awards, three American Music Awards, two MTV Video Music Awards, and the Allan Slaight Honour from Canada's Walk of Fame. He has been nominated for three Grammy Awards and one Brit Award.

CHAPTER TWO

Cinema of Canada

- **Cinema of Canada**

Cinema in Canada dates back to the earliest known display of film in Saint-Laurent, Quebec, in 1896. The film industry in Canada has been dominated by the United States, which has utilized Canada as a shooting location and to bypass British film quota laws, throughout its history. Canadian filmmakers, English and French, have been active in the development of cinema in the United States.

Films by Thomas A. Edison, Inc. were some of the first to arrive in Canada and early films made in the country were produced by Edison Studios. Canadian Pacific Railway and other railways supported early filmmaking including James Freer, whose Ten Years in Manitoba was the first known film by a Canadian. Evangeline is the earliest recorded Canadian feature film. George Brownridge and Ernest Shipman were major figures in Canadian cinema in the 1920s and 1930s. Shipman oversaw the production the most expensive film up to that point. Brownridge's career led to Carry on, Sergeant! and its failure caused a decline in the film industry.

The Canadian Government Motion Picture Bureau was formed in 1918, and expanded to sound and 16 mm film in the 1930s before merging into the National Film Board of Canada. The NFB expanded under the leadership of John Grierson. The Canadian Cooperation Project between the government and Motion Picture Association of America from 1948 to 1958, negatively effected Canadian filmmaking. Internal divisions between English and French Canadians within the NFB starting in the 1940s led to the creation of an independent branch for French language productions by the 1960s. The government provided financial support to the film industry through the Capital Cost Allowance and Telefilm Canada.

- **Arrival of film**

A film showing by Andrew M. Holland and George C. Holland was incorrectly viewed as the first in Canadian history until 1984. Their showing was conducted in West End Park, Ottawa (pictured 1892).

The first time a film was displayed in Canada, and one of the first times in North America, was at an event organized by Louis Minier and Louis Pupier using a cinematograph in Saint-Laurent, Quebec, on 27 June 1896. Prior to the discovery of the Saint-Laurent showing by Germain Lacasse in 1984, it was believed that a showing conducted by Andrew M. Holland and George C. Holland, where films by Thomas A. Edison, Inc. such as The Kiss were shown, in Ottawa, on 21 July 1896, was the first. The Saint-Laurent showing was overlooked as English researchers did not search through French sources. Léo-Ernest Ouimet stated that he attended the showing and he was used as evidence of it until Lacasse found newspaper coverage of the event in La Presse.

The development of a Canadian film industry was hampered by the country's low population density, it had six million inhabitants and only Toronto and Montreal had more than 100,000 people in 1905, and the lack of domestic vaudeville as most of the acts came from the United States, United Kingdom, and France. Early films were used to as promotional material for companies, promote immigration, or displays of scenic locations including Niagara Falls. The Edison Company created some of the first films in Canada by documenting the Klondike Gold Rush, Canadian soldiers leaving to fight in the Second Boer War, and George V, the Duke of York, arriving in Canada in 1902.

- **Charles Urban's Bioscope Company of Canada in 1903**

James Freer is believed to have been the first Canadian to produce films. He purchased an Edison camera and projector and started filming agriculture activates and Canadian Pacific Railway trains in 1897, and toured the United Kingdom with the sponsorship of the CPR in 1898, and a second less successful tour was sponsored by Clifford Sifton in 1901. His second tour was the first time that the government was directly involved with film. British and American filmmakers were selected as they could guarantee the distribution of their films unlike Canadian filmmakers. The CPR enlisted Charles Urban and his company, in order to allow the distribution of the films to the United Kingdom, to travel and film Canada to promote settlement in the western areas. This group, the Bioscope Company of Canada, conducted filming in Quebec to Victoria from 1902 to 1903.

The film, Living Canada, was premiered at the Palace Theatre in 1903, with High Commissioner Donald Smith in attendance. A total of thirty-five Living Canada films were released by 1904, and was reedited into Wonders of Canada in 1906. Urban success led to him gaining contracts with the government of British Columbia and the Northern Railway Company. The Grand Trunk Railway entered the industry by hiring Butcher's Film Service in 1909. The CPR hired the Edison Company to film in Canada and they sent nine people, including J. Searle Dawley, Henry Cronjager, and Mabel Trunnelle, in 1910. They were provided a specialized train and the RMS Empress of India and produced thirteen films.

- **Creating an independent film industry**

Silent films used intertitles in English and French, but sound films were mostly produced in English. The first recorded feature film created in Canada was Evangeline. The Palace was the first theatre to transition to showing sound films when it presented Street Angel on 1 September 1928. There were multiple attempts to create an independent film industry in Canada in the early 20th century. Thirty-six companies meant for film production were created between 1914 and 1922, but the majority of the companies did not produce any films.

The title card of British Canadian Pathe News as presented by Léo-Ernest Ouimet's Specialty Film Import.In 1914, Canadian Animated Weekly by Universal Pictures became one of the first newsreels in Canada. Ouimet, who was a pioneer for Canadian newsreels, created Specialty Film Import in 1915, as a distributor, but his newsreel and distribution companies were sold in 1923, and he unsuccessfully worked in the United States in the 1920s. At the peak of Ouimet's career 1.5 million Canadians were watching his newsreels twice per week. Domestic newsreel companies were unsuccessful after branches of American companies, Fox Canadian News and Canadian Kinograms, were established.

Ernest Shipman established multiple film companies in cities and would produce a limited amount of films using local money before moving to another area. Unlike other Canadian filmmakers he sought financial support from the American market. In 1919, incorporated Canadian Photoplays with a financial capital of $250,000 in Alberta. He started production on Wapi, the Walrus, but retitled it to Back to God's Country to capitalize God's Country and the Woman, starring his wife Nell Shipman.

The film was a critical and financial success, with it grossing over $500,000 in its first year, and Shipman's investors saw a 300% return on investment. Despite the success of the film Canadian Photoplays did not produce another film and went into voluntary liquidation. He signed a contract with Ralph Connor in 1919, and formed Dominion Films, based in New York, to produce films in Winnipeg. Winnipeg Productions was formed to adapt twelve of Connor's stories, but only five were filmed. Shipman created five companies across Canada in 1922, but only three produced films. He incorporated New Brunswick Films on 23 August 1922, but the failure of Blue Water ended Shipman's career.

Trenton, Ontario, despite its small size, was a major film production area and had one of the few studios to last longer than a few years. Canadian National Features, founded by George Brownridge, construction a studio in the town and raised a financial capital of $500,000, with

$278,000 coming within the first week, in 1916. However, the company suspended production after spending $43,000 on its first two films, The Marriage Trap and Power, and declared bankruptcy with $79,000 in assets. The studio in Trenton was taken over by the Pan American Film Corporation in 1918, but only released one film before closing. Brownridge founded Adanac Producing Company and released the two Canadian National Features films in 1918.

Brownridge shifted production towards corporate sponsorships by displaying products in dramatized films. Brownridge sought a sponsorship from the CPR and John Murray Gibbon saw Power and asked Brownridge to make anti-Bolshevik films during the First Red Scare. Adanac was reorganized in 1919, with Brownridge as its managing director and Denis Tansey, a member of parliament, as its president. The Great Shadow was released in 1920, after being filmed in Canada rather than New York as Brownridge wanted to create a domestic film industry, and was a critical and financial success although the CPR pulled its public support before its release. However, the company went bankrupt with Brownridge balming Harley Knoles's wastefulness and Selznick Pictures's distribution policy. Brownridge sold the Trenton studio to the Ontario Motion Picture Bureau in 1924, and it continued to be used, with Carry on, Sergeant! as the sole fictional work filmed there, until Mitchell Hepburn ordered its closure in 1934, and it was turned into a community centre.

British Columbia's government agencies used promotional films from 1908 to 1919, before the creation of the British Columbia Patriotic and Educational Picture Service. It was headed by May Watkis, who was the first woman to lead a film agency in Canada. Specialty Film

Import was the distributor for the service and the provincial legislature passed legislation requiring the display of at least one ten-minute education film or travelogue during all of the programs. The Motion Picture Branch of the Bureau of Publications was created by Saskatchewan in 1924, to produce education films.

The Ontario Motion Picture Bureau was established in 1917, but did not produce its own films until 1923. S.C. Johnson, who worked in the Ontario Agriculture Department, was its first director. The victory of the United Farmers of Ontario in the 1919 election resulted in Peter Smith reorganized film production under the Amusement Branch with Otter Elliott heading it. He changed the focus of filmmaking from agricultural training towards quality productions. By 1925, the bureau had 2,000 films in its library, distributed 1,500 reels of film per month, and made one feature-length documentary, Cinderella of the Farms in 1931, but the bureau was dissolved after the Ontario Liberal Party won in the 1934 Ontario general election.

Albert Tessier and Maurice Proulx produced large amounts of films in French at a time when it was uncommon. Joseph Morin, the Quebec Minister of Agriculture, used film for education purposes and the Service de ciné-photographie was established in 1941.

The Associated Screen News of Canada was founded by Bernard Norrish in 1920, and the CPR held a majority control of its stock. The company grew from two employees in 1920, to over one hundred by 1930, and focused on the production of newsreels, theatrical shorts, and sponsored films. It was one of Canada's longest lasting film production companies with Crawley Films and the National Film Board of Canada being one of the few to outlast it. Before ASN constructed a film laboratory all of the film print distributed in Canada were processed in the United States. The company was processing twenty-two million feet of film in per year by 1929. ASN constructed a sound stage in 1936, and produced House in Order, which was its only feature film in the 1930s.

Carry on, Sergeant! was a major film production in the late 1920s. Its failure resulted in a decline of the Canadian film industry that it did not recover from until after World War II.Brownridge was sent to New York in 1925 by the Ontario Motion Picture Bureau to gain a distribution contract, but only negotiated one with Cranfield and Clarke after a year of high expenses. Treasurer William Herbert Price criticized Brownridge stating that his "travelling expenses are very high and I do not see there was very much result from anything he has done".

George Patton, the bureau's head, supported the deal as Cranfield and Clarke had no Jews in its company. W.F. Clarke, who was later blamed for the company's financial failure, pushed for Canadian film production and came up with an idea of a film about "a dramatic story written by an eminent authority around the part played by the Canadians in the World War". Clarke incorporated British Empire Films of Canada in June 1927. The film adaption of The Better 'Ole was released in Canada under the name Carry On! and was financially success. Clarke's film was named Carry on, Sergeant! to help raise funds. It received financial backing from influential people, including prime ministers Arthur Meighen and Bennett. The film started production, by the recently created subsidiary Canadian International Films, in 1926, and Bruce Bairnsfather was hired to direct with an expensive contract, but his inexperience with film led to production troubles that increased the cost of the budget. The production difficulties led to internal company problems and Clarke was removed as general manager although he remained vice-president.

The film was released in 1928, to mixed-to-negative reviews and was only distributed in Ontario before the company went bankrupt in 1929. Brownridge attempted to recut and release the film in 1930, stating that it "would gross at least $200,000", but it did not happen. The Ontario government was still interested in attempting to create a large film studio by 1932, along with Edward Wentworth Beatty and Herbert Samuel Holt, but the recent failure of Canadian International Films and Great Depression led to its not receiving investments. The Canadian film industry would not recover until after World War II.

- **National Film Board**

A group of cameramen who worked for the Canadian Government Motion Picture Bureau in 1925. Frank Badgley, the bureau's director from 1927 to 1941, is in the background.The Exhibits and Publicity Bureau was founded on 19 September 1918, and was reorganized into the Canadian Government Motion Picture Bureau in 1923. The organization's budget stagnated and declined during the Great Depression. Frank Badgley, who served as the bureau's director from 1927 to 1941, stated that the bureau needed to transition to sound films or else it would lose its access to theatrical releases, but the organization did not gain the equipment until 1934, and by then it had lost its theatrical distributors. Badgley was able to get a 16 mm film facility for the bureau in 1931. The bureau was reorganized into the National Film Board of Canada in 1941, following John Grierson's recommendation.

Ross McLean was working as the secretary to High Commissioner Vincent Massey when he met Grierson, and asked for Grierson to come to Canada to aide in the governmental film policy. Grierson made a report on the Canadian film industry in 1938, and the National Film Act, which he drafted, was passed in 1939 causing the creation of the NFB. Grierson became the first Film Commissioner of the NFB and served until the end of World War II. Employment rose from fifty to over seven hundred from 1941 to 1945, although it was cut by 40% after the war ended. Grierson selected McLean to work as assistant commissioner and Stuart Legg to oversee the productions.

Grierson made efforts to increase the theatrical distribution of NFB films, primarily its war-related films, as he was coordinating wartime information for the United Kingdom in North America. Famous Players aided in distribution and the Canadian Motion Picture War Services Committee, which worked with the War Activities Committee of the Motion Pictures Industry, was founded in 1940. NFB productions such as The World in Action was watched by 30-40 million people per month in the United Kingdom and United States in 1943, and Canada Carries On was watched by 2.25 million people by 1944. The audience for NFB newsreels reached 40-50 million per week by 1944.

Grierson opposed feature film production as he believed that Canada did not have a large enough market for an independent feature film industry. He supported working with American film companies and stated that "the theatre film business is an international business, dependent when it comes to distribution on an alliance or understanding with American film interests". He travelled to Hollywood in 1944, and the NFB sent scripts to American companies for consideration.

Grierson lacked strong support in the Canadian government and some of his films received opposition from members of the government. Inside Fighting Russia was criticized for its support of the Russian Revolution and Balkan Powderkeg for criticizing the United Kingdom's policy in the Balkans. Grierson and the NFB were attacked during the onset of the Cold War. The Federal Bureau of Investigation created a file on Grierson in 1942, due to the World in Action newsreel being considered too left-wing. Leo Dolan, an ally of Hepburn and the head of the Canadian Government Travel Bureau, accused Grierson of being Jewish and a Co-operative Commonwealth Federation supporter. The Gouzenko Affair implicated Freda Linton, one of Grierson's secretaries, and the organization was criticized by the Progressive Conservative Party for subversive tendencies, financial waste, and being a monopoly. Grierson was also accused of being involved, but was proven not to be although he resigned as commissioner in 1945.

McLean was ordered to assist the Royal Canadian Mounted Police screen NFB employees and the RCMP requested him to fire a list of employees. McLean, who refused to fire any employees without their disloyalty being proven, was not reappointed as commissioner and replaced by William Arthur Irwin in 1950. Irwin also refused to fire employees without proven disloyalty and reduced the demand and only three of the thirty-six requested were fired.

The Royal Commission on National Development in the Arts, Letters and Sciences, with Massey as its chair, was formed in 1949. The NFB submitted a brief asking to have a headquarters constructed, budget increases, and to become a Crown corporation. Robert Winters, whose ministry oversaw the NFB, stated that its brief did not represent government policy. The Association of Motion Picture Producers and Laboratories of Canada submitted a brief criticizing a government monopoly, with the NFB's crown corporation request being referred to as an "expansionist, monopolistic psychology", and that they were unable to compete with the NFB as it paid no taxes and was exempt from tariffs. The commission's report supported the NFB and its requests for Crown corporation status and a headquarters were accepted.

The financial success of Royal Journey, depicting Princess Elizabeth and Prince Philip's tour of Canada, aided the NFB and was one of the reasons that John Grierson said that William Arthur Irwin "saved the Film Board".

A Canadian tour by Princess Elizabeth and Prince Philip was filmed and was initially meant to be two reels, worth twenty minutes, but grew to five reels as they could not determine what to cut. Irwin met with Harvey Harnick, the NFB's Columbia theatrical distributor, and J.J. Fitzgibbons, the president of Famous Players, and Fitzgibbons told Irwin that he would screen all five reels if the film was completed for a Christmas release. Royal Journey opened in seventeen first-run theatres and over course of the next two years it was screened in 1,249 Canadian theatres where it was watched by a record two million people and the film was also screened in forty other countries. The film cost $88,000, but the NFB gained a profit of $150,000 and the film's success was one of the reasons Grierson stated that Irwin "saved the Film Board".

The Canadian Government Motion Picture Bureau and Associated Screen News of Canada had no French-Canadian employees. Vincent Paquette became the NFB's first French-Canadian filmmaker in 1941, and directed La

Cité de Notre-Dame, the board's first in-house French-language film, in 1942. The number of French-Canadian employees grew to seventeen by 1945, and a quarter of the board's budget was spent on French productions. The Massey Commission and Gratien Gélinas, a member of the NFB's Board of Governors, called for an improvement in French-language productions, but Premier Maurice Duplessis opposed it.

French-language media, including Le Devoir, criticized the NFB after it removed Roger Blais in 1957. NFB francophone directors Denys Arcand, Gilles Carle, Jacques Godbout, Gilles Groulx, and Clément Perron criticized the organization for its censorship policies, refusal to produce feature films, and its colonial treatment of Quebec. Michel Brault, Carle, Bernard Gosselin, Groulx, and Arthur Lamothe left following reprimands. Guy Roberge became the first French-Canadian to serve as the NFB's commissioner. Duplessis died in 1959, and Quebec Liberal Party gained control while the Liberal Party won in the 1963 Canadian federal election. The Liberals supported a policy of bilingualism and biculturalism. A French-language branch of the NFB that was independent of its English-language productions was formed in 1964, under the leadership of Pierre Juneau.

Drylanders, the organization's first English language feature-length fiction film, was released in 1963.Kathleen Shannon organized Studio D, the first publicly funded feminist film-production unit in the world, in 1974, and produced 125 films before its closure in 1996. However, there would be no French version of Studio D until the formation of Studio B in 1986.

- **Governmental financial involvement**

Starting in 1954, the Capital Cost Allowance was able to be used for a 60% tax write-off for film investment and the amount was increased to 100% in 1974. $1.2 billion was invested in Canadian film and television in the thirteen years following the increase. The average film budget rose from $527,000 to $2.6 million in 1979, and $3.5 million in 1986. From 1958 to 1967, private film investment accounted for 18% of film investments and it declined to 13.5% in 1968, while the CFDC accounted for 37.5%. Following the tax write-off increase private investment rose to account for 47% of film investment between 1975 and 1978 while the CFDC declined to 15%. Silence of the North was the first film with American backing to receive CCA certification. The Film and Video Production Tax Credit replaced the Capital Cost Allowance in 1995.

In 1962, Roberge proposed the creation of an organization to aid in film finance based on the National Film Finance Corporation and Centre national du cinéma et de l'image animée.

- **Norman Jewison founded the Canadian Film Centre**

The Interdepartmental Committee on the Possible Development of a Feature Film Industry in Canada, under the leadership of NFB commissioner Roberge, was formed by the secretary of state. The committee submitted a report to the 19th Canadian Ministry for the creation of a loan fund to aid the development of the Canadian film industry. The proposal was approved in October 1965, and legislation, the Canadian Film Development Corporation Act of 1966-67, for its creation was introduced in June 1966, before being approved on 3 March 1967. The Canadian Film Development Corporation was established with a budget of $10 million in 1967. In February 1968, Spender was appointed as its director along with a five-member board. Canada lack of a film school leading to the creation of the Canadian Film Centre by Norman Jewison. The CFDC started investing up to 50% of its budget into films that cost less than $500,000.

Explosion was the first film to receive financial support from the CFDC. Valérie by Denis Héroux, which was not financially supported by the CFDC, was made at cost of $70,000 and made over $1 million in Quebec. The CDFC financially supported Héroux's other films Here and Now, Love in a Four-Letter World, Virgin Lovers, and Deux Femmes en or. Deux Femmes en or was financially successful, with its two million ticket sales remaining the highest in Canadian history, and became the highest grossing Canadian film.

The $10 million budget was used by October 1971, after the CFDC invested $6.7 million into 64 films with an average cost of $250,000 per film. The CFDC was not financially successful as only three of those films made a profit and the organization recovered $600,000 of its investments. After 1970 the CFDC focused on investing in smaller budgeted films and ended its work with American theatrical distributors to them hiding profits. Another $10 million budget was given to the CFDC in November 1971, and a new investment strategy in which $600,000 per year would be invested into productions, with its creative and technical crew being Canadian, budgeted below $100,000, and $3 million per year on films with guaranteed distribution.

It took the CFDC five years to recover its first $1 million investment, but recovered $1 million in 1977 alone. From 1977 to 1978, the CFDC invested $1.6 million into twenty films and its investments rose to $10.8 million into 34 films from 1979 to 1980. Between 1968 and 1978, the organization funded 103 English-language films, but only Black Christmas, Death Weekend, Heart Farm, Shivers, and The Apprenticeship of Duddy Kravitz were profitable to the CFDC.

The Toronto Filmmakers' Coop, an organization with 150 filmmakers, sent a letter with the endorsement of 200 filmmakers to Gérard Pelletier asking for the creation of a content quota that required distributors to have 15% of their films be Canadian. Pelletier announced the creation of a theatre in the National Capital Region that exclusively showed Canadian films in 1972. A study published by the Secretary of State reported that a content quota would not work as a 50% quote would generate less revenue than a 5% sales increase for foreign films. The study stated that new tax regulations and investments by the CFDC could make the Canadian film industry internationally competitive.

The budget for the CFDC was limited to a few million and its budget from 1982 to 1983 was $4.5 million. However, the organization had its role expanded to include television in 1983, and administered the Canadian Broadcast Program Development Fund. The television fund was initially given an annual budget of $60 million. An annual budget of $30 million through the Feature Film Fund was created in 1986, and an annual budget of $17 million through the Feature Film Distribution Fund was created in 1988. The organization's combined budget grew to $146 million by 1989.

A report was written by a task force in 1985, and it stated that foreign domination of film and video distribution, chronic undercapitalization of production companies, and concentration of theatre ownership and distribution and exhibition vertical integration hurt the development of the film industry. They recommended legislation to increase the control of Canadian-owned companies over distribution and Minister of Communications Flora MacDonald proposed a film licensing system based on their recommendations. American distributors opposed the policy and lobbied the American government through the MPAA and its president, Jack Valenti. Valenti met with President Ronald Reagan at least twice and Reagan criticized the legislation of a US-Canadian economic summit. 54 members of the United States Congress signed a letter to Prime Minister Brian Mulroney opposing the legislation. The legislation was not tabled and it failed.

- **Post-Carry on, Sergeant**

F. R. Crawley, who was involved in filmmaking for a decade, and Judith Crawley created Île d'Orléans in 1938, and its success led to a $3,000 loan from F. R. Crawley's father that created Crawley Films. It employment rose from 6 in 1946, 33 in 1949, and around 100 by the 1950s. One-sixth of the $3 million worth of films produced by the Canadian film industry in 1952 came from Crawley Films.

France Film and other companies started creating French film productions in the 1930s. Maria Chapdelaine is commonly, although incorrectly, regarded as the first French-Canadian sound movie. Étienne Brûlé gibier de potence was the first colour feature film made in Quebec and the first Canadian colour film shot in English and French. Joseph-Alexandre DeSève monopolized the distribution of French-language films through France-Film. France-Film arose from the distribution of Maria

Chapdelaine which sold 70,000 tickets in Canada. He also aided in the production of Notre-Dame de la Mouise in response to the papal encyclical Vigilanti Cura. DeSève purchased Renaissance Films following the success of The Music Master. DeSève produced four films through Renaissance Films Distribution. Paul L'Anglais formed Quebec Productions filmed Whispering City in English and French, under the title La Forteresse. It was seen by over 100,000 people in Quebec over the course of six weeks.

The papal encyclical Vigilanti Cura in 1936, changed the Catholic attitude towards movies and the church became a part of Quebec movie production in the 1940s. Most of the nineteen movies, fifteen in French and four in English, produced in Quebec from 1944 to 1953 were made by Renaissance Films or Quebec Productions.Bush Pilot was the only English-language feature film created by a Canadian company in the 1940s.

- **Modern industry**

Canadians had to import colour 35 mm film until 1967, as Canada did not produce any internally.By the 1960s Nat Taylor, a theatre owner, controlled the largest private film studio in Canada, Toronto International Film Studios, two distribution companies, International Film Distributors and Allied Artists Pictures, a television station, CJOH-DT, and multiple production companies. He entered film production with The Mask in 1961. Taylor, unlike other members of the AMPPLC, supported state involvement in feature film production.

Bryant Fryer founded one of the first animation companies in Canada and made six silhouette films from 1927 to 1935. Norman McLaren was brought to Canada from Scotland by Grierson in 1941. McLaren recruited English-Canadian animators from OCAD University, including George Dunning, Evelyn Lambart, Grant Munro, and Robert Verrall. McLaren recruited French-Canadian animators from École des beaux-arts de Montréal, including René Jodoin. Jodoin created a French animation unit in 1966, which included Laurent Coderre and Bernard Longpré. Le village enchanté was the first recorded animated feature film in Canadian history and Return to Oz which was based on Tales of the Wizard of Oz, the first recorded Canadian animated television series, was the second recorded animated feature film.

In the 1960s filmmakers came from universities throughout Canada. David Cronenberg, Clarke Mackey, and David Secter graduated from the University of Toronto. John Hofsess, Ivan Reitman, and Peter Rowe graduated from McMaster University. Jack Darcus and Larry Kent graduated from the University of British Columbia. Cronenberg received financial support from the CFDC and Shivers was their most successful investment, with a budget of $150,000 ($75,000 from the CFDC) and gross of $5 million. 708 feature films, over twice the amount made in the past fifty years, were made during the 1970s.

Carle, Groulx, Claude Jutra, and Jean Pierre Lefebvre, who were inspired by the French New Wave, made their directorial debuts from 1963 to 1965, and all won the Grand Prix at the Montreal International Film Festival throughout the 1960s. Jean-Claude Lauzon's Night Zoo won the most Genie Awards in history, with thirteen awards.

Porky's became the first Canadian film to gross more than $100 million. The Care Bears Movie, by Nelvana, was the highest-grossing non-Disney animated film at the time of its release. Six of the ten highest-grossing films in Canada between 1991 to 2001, were made in Quebec.

- **Theatres**

In the 1890s and 1900s films were shown by travelling showmen. John C. Green, a magician who presented for the Holland brothers at their first showing, travelled throughout eastern Canada and New England until the establishment of movie theatres. John Albert Schuberg was credited with bringing movies to Vancouver and Winnipeg, and the provinces of British Columbia and the Canadian Prairies. Schuberg established Canada's first permanent movie theatre, the Electric Theatre, in Vancouver, in October 1902, with its first movie played being The Eruption of Mount Pelee. He opened additional theatres in Winnipeg, and later gained the license for First National Pictures in western Canada. He had one of the largest theatre chains and sold it to Jay and Jules Allen in 1919, before returning in 1921, and then selling it to Famous Players in 1924.

Jay and Jules Allen established their first theatre in Brantford in 1906. The established Allen Amusement Corporation, a film exchange, in 1908. Their chain was worth over $20 million by 1920, and had fifty-three theatres by 1923, when they declared bankruptcy and it was acquired by Famous Players. The Allens owned the distribution rights for Pathé and Paramount Pictures. In 1916, they rejected an offer by Paramount president Adolph Zukor to create an equal partnership. The Allens informed Nathan Nathanson of this attempt and Nathanson convinced Zukor to give him their distribution rights in 1920, for twenty years after creating his own theatre chain.Nathan Nathanson founded Famous Players and

Odeon Theatres. These companies controlled the theatre industry in Canada.

Nathanson's Famous Players started an expansion campaign in the 1920s that led to its gaining control of all first run theatres in the major cities. Zukor and Paramount forced Nathanson out of Famous Players after buying a large amount of the stock in 1930. Famous Players also controlled the distribution industry in Canada, accounting for at least 40% of distribution, due to its connections to Paramount Pictures. Paul Nathanson managed Regal Films, which was controlled by Paramount, and distributed films from British International Pictures, Metro-Goldwyn-Mayer, and Pathé, and Famous Players also distributed films from Columbia Pictures. Fox Film, RKO Pictures, Tiffany Pictures, and Warner Bros. were the other main distributors in Canada in the 1930s. A study conducted by United Artists in 1931 showed that 67% of rental revenue in Canada came from nineteen theatres in Canada's main cities while the remainder came from the rest.

Block booking by major studios, that were from outside Canada, prevented independent theatre owners from obtaining films at a reasonable price. R. B. Bennett, who invested into the film industry, made investigating the film industry an issue in the 1930 election. Peter White was appointed to investigate Famous Players' monopolistic control of theatres under the Combines Investigation Act. White concluded that "a combine exists and has existed at least since the year of 1926" and Famous Players was detrimental to the public interest in 1931, but no action was taken against the company. Bennett supported taking action and the attorney generals of Alberta, British Columbia, Ontario, and Saskatchewan would prosecute Famous Players. Fifteen companies and three people, including Nathan Nathanson, were charged, but the Supreme Court of Canada ruled in favor of the companies.

After losing control over Famous Players Nathanson created Odeon Theatres in April 1941, and resigned from his position at Famous Players in May. He built the company using Regal Films, which was managed by his brother and distributed MGM films, and gaining the business of companies whose contracts with Famous Players were expiring. Odeon did not gain a MGM distribution contract, but did gain ones for all of Columbia Pictures' films, two-thirds of Universal's films, and one-third of Fox's films. Nathanson died in 1943, and was succeeded by his son Paul. Films released in Famous Players and Odeon theatres, both foreign owned after Paul sold his stock to J. Arthur Rank in 1946, accounted for over 60% of the Canadian box office by 1947.

Taylor, who declined to become the general manager of Odeon in 1941, founded Twentieth Century Theatres in the 1930s and the Famous Players-aligned company grew to own sixty-five theatres by the 1960s. He opened the International Theatre in Toronto which was the first theatre in Canada dedicated towards screening art films. Taylor and Garth Drabinsky created the Cineplex Odeon Corporation in 1979, and by 1987 it was the largest theatre chain in North America with 1,500 theatres, with two-thirds of them in the United States.

The deaths of seventy-eight children from the Laurier Palace Theatre fire in 1927, and opposition to film from the Catholic Church led to a ban on minors attending movie theatres until 1961. In the 1930s Quebec was the only province that allowed for theatres to be open on Sundays.The Quebec Cinema Act, passed in 1983, required that English-language films in Quebec must be translated into French within sixty days. However, films from the United States were unaffected as their distribution ended before the deadline and the NFB was exempted from the requirements.

The Canadian box office increased following World War II. In 1934, there were 796 theatres which admitted 107 million people to earn $25 million and that grew to 1,229 theatres admitting 151 million people to make $37 million in 1940. By 1950, the amount of theatres increased to 2,360 earning $86 million with 245 million people attending. However, during the 1950s Canadian film attendance declined with the nation falling from the fifth-highest in film attendance to twenty-fifth by the 1960s and the amount of films the average Canadian saw per year dropped from seventeen in 1950 to eight in 1960. Ticket sales in Quebec fell from 60 million in 1952, to 19 million in 1969. The amount of theatres in Canada declined from 1,635 in 1962, to 1,400 in 1967, to 1,116 in 1974, and to 899 in 1984.

- **International Canadian Hollywood**

Many native-born Canadians, such as Al Christie, Allan Dwan, Louis B. Mayer, Sidney Olcott, Mack Sennett, and Jack L. Warner, aided in the creation and development of the American film industry.

In the early 1900s Canada was used as a shooting location for dramatic productions with Hiawatha, the Messiah of the Ojibway being one of the first in 1903.The Kalem Company was one of the first American companies to conduct location shooting in Canada in 1909. Two of the films D. W. Griffith made in his first year as a director, The Ingrate and A Woman's Way, were made in Canada. British American Film Company, Canadian Bioscope Company,

Conness Till Film Company of Toronto, and the All-Red Feature Company, the four Canadians companies that produced fictional films prior to World War I, had their invested come from Americans, but all of them were financially unsuccessful and closed within a few years with Conness Till suffering a fire that destroyed their $50,000 studio.

Canadians were hostile to American filmmakers and provincial film review boards instituted censorship policies in 1915, which included a ban on the gratuitous display of the flag of the United States. Fifty reels of film were banned in British Columbia in 1914, due to "an unnecessary display of U.S. flags" which put it as the third most common reason behind infidelity and seduction. In 1927, the United Kingdom created a quota limiting the amount of foreign films that could be shown in the country, but productions that were produced within the British Empire and was mostly made by British subjects were excluded from the quotas. American financers produced low-budget B movies within Canada to exploit the loophole before the legislation was changed in 1938 to exclude the Dominion. Nanook of the North and The Viking exploited the loophole. From 1928 to 1938, twenty-two feature films, the majority of Canada's film production, meant solely for the British market were filmed.

American companies made $17 million in profits from Canada in 1947. Prime Minister William Lyon Mackenzie King's government sought to reduce the general trade imbalance between Canada and the United States. McLean called for the reinvestment of this money into Canadian film production and requiring the American distribution of Canadian shorts. The Motion Picture Association of America proposed the Canadian Cooperation Project and it was accepted by the Canadian government on 14 January 1948. The government would not restrict revenue to American companies in exchange for productions being filmed in Canada and mentions of Canada in those scripts to promote tourism. The project was considered unsuccessful and stifled Canadian filmmaking, with only eight Canadian feature films being made during the CCP's existence, before it ended in 1958. McLean was critical of the agreement as there was a lack of Canadian films distributed in the United States. Michael Spencer stated that the agreement was "allowed to die of embarrassment".

Gilbert Agar attended the Fourth National Motion Picture Conference of the Motion Picture Council in America in 1926, and reported that 95% of films released in Canada were from the United States. Eric Johnston stated that "outside the U.S. itself, Canada ranks as the second largest market in the world for Hollywood films." The amount of films in Canada of American origin declined to 68% by 1954, and 41% in 1962.

Canadian directors, such as Norman Jewison, left Canada to work in the United States. Raoul Barré worked as a cartoonist in Canada before moving to the United States and working as an animator at Barré Studio. Stephen Bosustow and other animators left Walt Disney Animation Studios during the Disney animators' strike and founded United Productions of America.

Seven Arts Productions, while being listed on the Toronto Stock Exchange and having a majority of its investors be Canadians, had the majority of its productions done by its American subsidiary. It spent $25 million on ten American film productions, including Dr. Strangelove and What Ever Happened to Baby Jane?. Canadian 3D animation companies, such as Softimage and Alias

Research, had their software used for American films, such as Jurassic Park.

Printed by Libri Plureos GmbH in Hamburg, Germany